Little Blue Dot

1

Sarah Dilger

Activity Book

OXFORD
UNIVERSITY PRESS

MODULE	UNIT	VOCABULARY	STRUCTURES	LETTERS & PHONICS	VALUES & FUNCTIONAL LANGUAGE	NUMBERS	EXPLORE	PROJECT
Let's talk p.4 Concept: *communication* hello, goodbye	**Unit 1 Hello** p.6 **Generalization:** *We can communicate with spoken words and different languages.*	dragon look, listen, sing, say yes, no	I'm (Lara). This is (Jake). What's your name? I'm a dragon!	The alphabet	**Be friendly** What's your name?	Days of the week	Listening games	Make finger puppets.
	Unit 2 My face p.16 **Generalization:** *We can communicate with our faces and body language.*	happy, sad, tired, angry hungry nose, mouth, eyes, ears monkey, lion	I'm (happy). I'm not (hungry). I have one (nose). I have two (eyes).	**a** (apple) **b** (bag) **c** (cat)	**Say sorry** Oh no! I'm sorry. That's okay.	1, 2	Animal body language	Make a self-portrait.
	Unit 3 Words and pictures p.26 **Generalization:** *We can communicate with written words and pictures.*	a crayon, a pencil, a book, an eraser red, pink, green, blue go, stop	I have (a crayon / an eraser). What's this? It's (a fish). It's (red).	**d** (door) **e** (egg) **f** (fish)	**Ask politely and say thank you** May I have (a book), please? Here you go. Thank you!	3, 4	Stop and go signs	Make a thank you card.
	Now I know Units 1–3 p.36							
	Story time: Let's play! p.38							
About us p.40 Concept: *identity* boy, girl	**Unit 4 My family** p.42 **Generalization:** *We live in family groups and these groups can take different forms.*	mom, dad, sister, brother grandma, grandpa, cousin, friend baby, me	This is my (mom). I don't have (a hoop). Who's this? She's/He's my (grandma / grandpa). This is me. I'm a baby.	**g** (game) **h** (hoop) **i** (insect)	**Take turns** It's my/your turn. Let's take turns.	5	Family photos	Make someone in your family.
	Unit 5 Me and my friends p.52 **Generalization:** *We have different abilities and these change as we grow.*	play, catch a ball, run, swim fly clap, cry, walk, talk share, help	I can (play). I can't (catch a ball). The baby can (clap). The baby can't (walk). I'm (friendly).	**j** (jump) **k** (kite) **l** (leaf)	**Help each other** Can you help, please? Sure!	Review 1–5	Friendship	Make a friendship badge.

MODULE	UNIT	VOCABULARY	STRUCTURES	LETTERS & PHONICS	VALUES & FUNCTIONAL LANGUAGE	NUMBERS	EXPLORE	PROJECT
About us **p.40** Concept: *identity* boy, girl	**Unit 6 We like food** **p.62** **Generalization:** *We like different things, and our likes and dislikes can change.*	bread, chocolate, cheese, salad milk, orange juice, lemonade, water bananas, watermelon	I like (bread). I don't like (cheese). May I have the chocolate, please? Do you like (milk)? Yes./No.	**m** (mango) **n** (noodles) **o** (olives)	**Keep trying new things** Try it, it's good! It's delicious!	6, 7	Fruit	Make a plate of food.
	Now I know Units 4–6 p.72							
	Story time: My mango! p.74							
	Unit 7 What's this? **p.78** **Generalization:** *We can categorize things by type and color.*	teddy bear, monster, balloon, doll triangle, rectangle, circle, square black, gray	What's this? It's a/an (orange) (teddy bear). It's my (blue) (robot). Don't worry. Where's the (green) (triangle)? Here it is.	**p** (purple) **q** (queen) **r** (robot)	**Be clean** What a mess! Let's clean up.	8, 9	Shapes in pictures	Print a shape picture.
Let's notice things p.76 Concept: *observation* different, the same	**Unit 8 What can we see?** **p.88** **Generalization:** *We can observe nature everywhere.*	tree, bird, stone, flower small, big, dirty, clean brown, white	I can see a/one (tree). I can see (two) (stones). I can't see (a dragon). I can see a (small) (cat). It's (brown).	**s** (sun) **t** (turtle) **u** (umbrella) **v** (volcano)	**Be careful** Be careful!	10	Insect camouflage	Make a print in salt-dough.
	Unit 9 Amazing animals **p.98** **Generalization:** *Different animals have different features and can do different things.*	goat, bee, dog, cow beautiful tail, head, legs, wings feathers, stripes	Is it a (goat)? Yes./No. It's beautiful! How many (dragons)? It has a (small) (tail). It has (two) (legs).	**w** (window) **x** (box) **y** (yellow) **z** (zebra)	**Don't touch wild animals** Don't touch the (bee)!	Review 1–10	Feathers	Decorate paper feathers to make a pair of wings.
	Now I know Units 7–9 p.108							
	Story time: The different duck p.110							

Let's talk

1 Look and match.

1 Choose one picture and draw yourself.

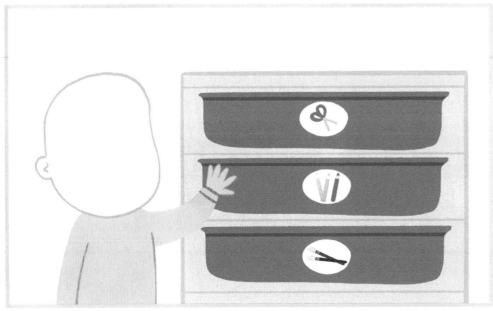

Hello

1 Trace.

1 🔊001 **Listen and point.** 2 🔊002 **Listen again and match.**

1 Trace and color.

S s

1 Look and match.

1 Who is being friendly? Look and circle.

Lesson 5 Value   **Value:** be friendly   **Language focus:** *What's your name?*

1 Point and say the days.   2 Draw yourself outside of school.

1 🔊003 Listen and point.　　2 Find the same picture and color.

Lesson 7 Song　　**Language focus:** *look, listen, sing, say*

1 Find the listening games and color the boxes.

1 Look and match.

Lesson 9 Project   **Language focus:** *This is (Spark).*

1 Look and color.   2  ◀))004 Listen and point.

My face

1 Trace.

005 Listen and circle.

2

1 Trace and say. 2 Color.

What's different? Circle four things.

1 Look. What's next? Choose and color 🙂.

Lesson 5 Value   **Value:** say sorry   **Language focus:** *Oh no! I'm sorry. That's okay.*

Look and color.

1

2

1 🔊006 Listen and color.

1 Point and say.   2 Think and color.

1 Look and think. Color the circles to match.

Lesson 9 Project   **Language focus:** *I'm (Lara). I have two (eyes).*

1 Look and match.   2 🔊007 Listen and point.

Words and pictures

1 Trace in **blue** to connect the words and **yellow** to connect the pictures.

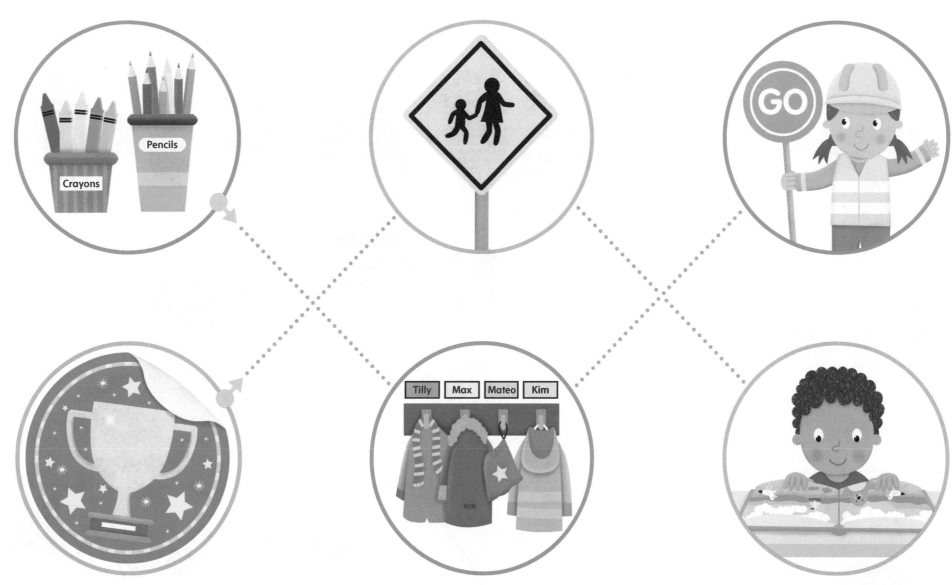

1 Trace and color.   2 🔊008 Listen and point.

3

1 Trace and say.   2 Look and match.

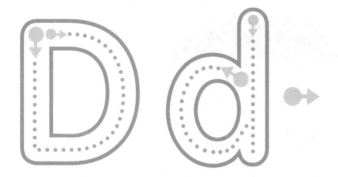

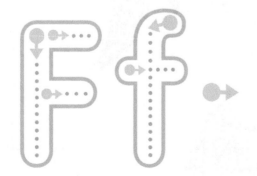

Do you remember? Look and color.

To Mom
Thank you!
from Spark

Language focus: *Here you go. Thank you!* Lesson 4 Story

3

1 Color the correct picture.

Value: ask politely and say thank you   **Language focus:** *May I have (a book), please? Here you go. Thank you!*

1 Count and color the number.

3

1 🔊009 Listen and match.

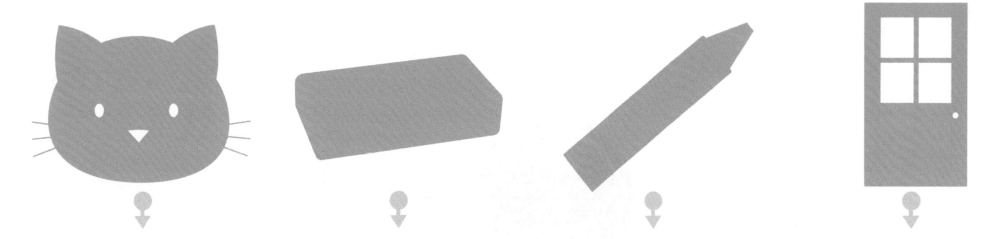

Lesson 7 Song   **Language focus:** *What's this? It's (a fish). It's red / pink / green / blue.*

1 Look and color **red** or green.

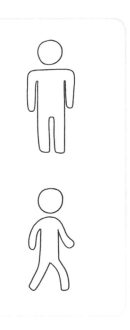

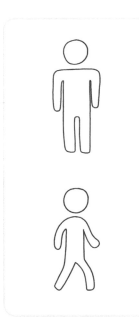

3

1 Look and match.

1 Look and color. 2  010 Listen and point.

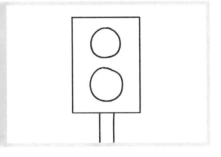

Unit 3 generalization: We can communicate with written words and pictures. Lesson 10 Review 35

Let's talk   Now I know

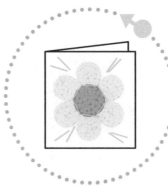

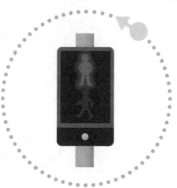

1 Who is being welcoming? Look and circle.

1 Trace and color.

2 Do you like the story? Color.

1 Choose one picture and draw yourself.

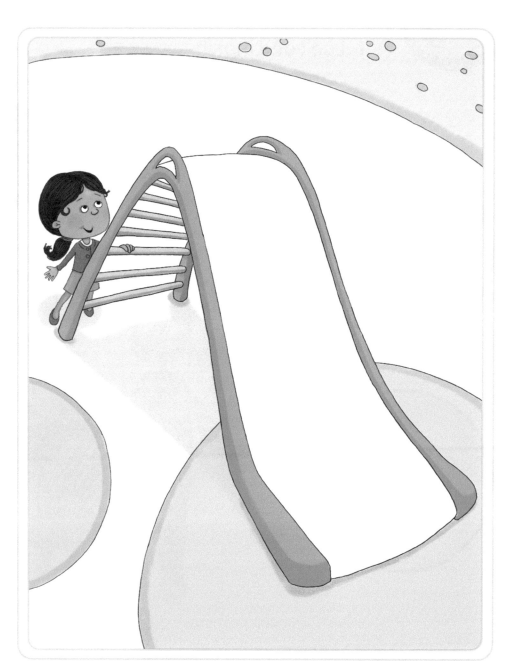

About us

1 Look and match.

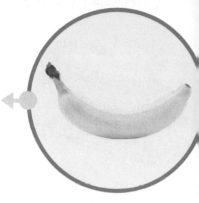

1 Choose one picture and draw yourself.

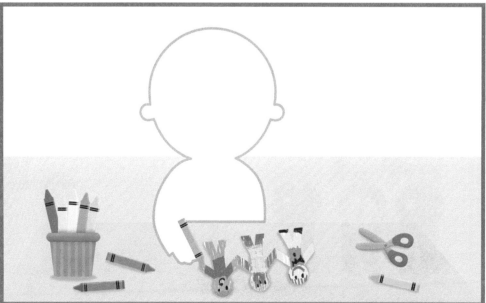

My family

1 Find the families and color the boxes.

1 🔊011 Listen and point. **2** 🔊012 Listen and circle.

4

1 Trace and say.

  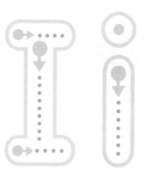

2 Look and circle.

1 What's different in picture 2? Circle four things.

1 Look. What's next? Choose and color ☺.

Lesson 5 Value   **Value:** take turns   **Language focus:** *It's my/your turn. Let's take turns.*

1 Look and draw.

5 ◯ ◯ ◯ ◯ ◯

5 ▢ ▢ ▢ ▢ ▢

1 🔊013 Listen and match.

Lesson 7 Song   **Language focus:** *Who's this? She's/He's my grandma / grandpa / cousin / friend.*

1 Look and connect the photos. Circle the boy in **red** and the girl in green.

1 Look and think. Color the circles to match.

1 Look and match. **2** 🔊014 Listen and point.

 # Me and my friends

1 Look. Color the circles to match.

1 🔊 015 Listen and match.

5

1 Trace and say.

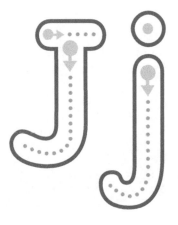

2 Look and match.

Lesson 3 Phonics   **Language focus:** initial letter sounds *j (jump), k (kite), l (leaf)*

1 Do you remember? Follow and circle the pictures in the story.

1 Who is helping? Look and circle.

Lesson 5 Value   **Value:** help each other   **Language focus:** *Can you help, please? Sure!*

1 Look and color.

1	
2	
3	
4	
5	

5

1 🔊016 Listen and point. **2** 🔊017 Listen again and color the ✓ or the ✗.

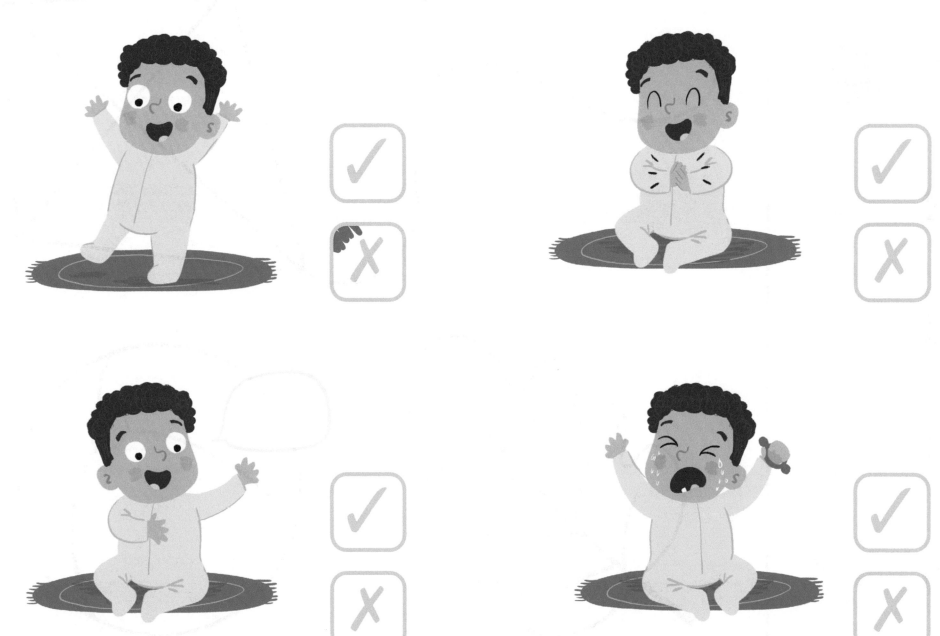

Lesson 7 Song   **Language focus:** *The baby can clap / cry. The baby can't walk / talk.*

1 Who is being a good friend? Look and match to ☺ or ☹.

1 Look, match, and color in **red** or green.

Lesson 9 Project   **Language focus:** *I can (share).*

5

1 Look and color.　**2** 🔊018 Listen and point.

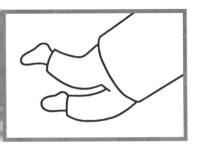

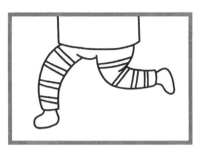

We like food

1 Look and match.   **2** Which foods do you like?

1 🔊 019 Listen and point.   **2** 🔊 020 Listen and circle.

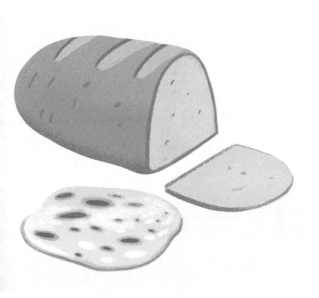

Language focus: *I like bread / chocolate. I don't like cheese / salad.*   **Lesson 2** Game   63

1 Trace and say.

2 Look and circle.

n　o　m

o　n　m

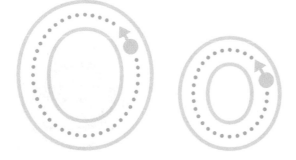

m　o　n

Language focus: initial letter sounds *m (mango)*, *n (noodles)*, *o (olives)*

1 Do you remember what's in Spark's sandwich? Look and color.

6

1 Look and draw 😊 and 😧.   **2** Color the 😊 picture.

1 Count and color.

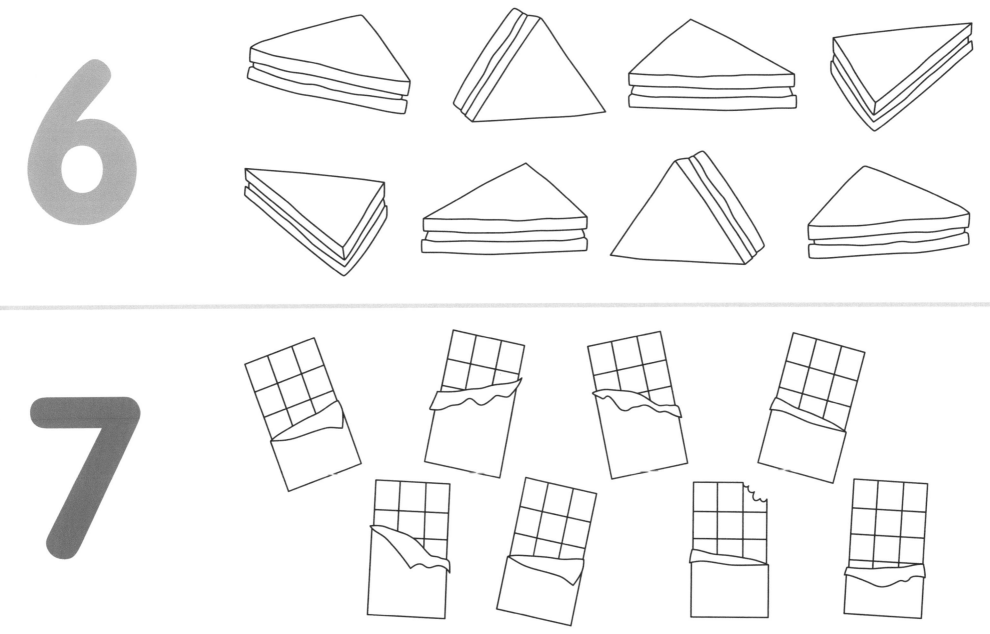

6

1 Trace.   **2** 🔊021 Listen and draw ☺ or ☹.

Lesson 7 Song   **Language focus:** *Do you like milk / orange juice / lemonade / water? Yes./No.*

1 Which fruit is the boy eating? Circle.

6

1 Which food is missing? Look and color.

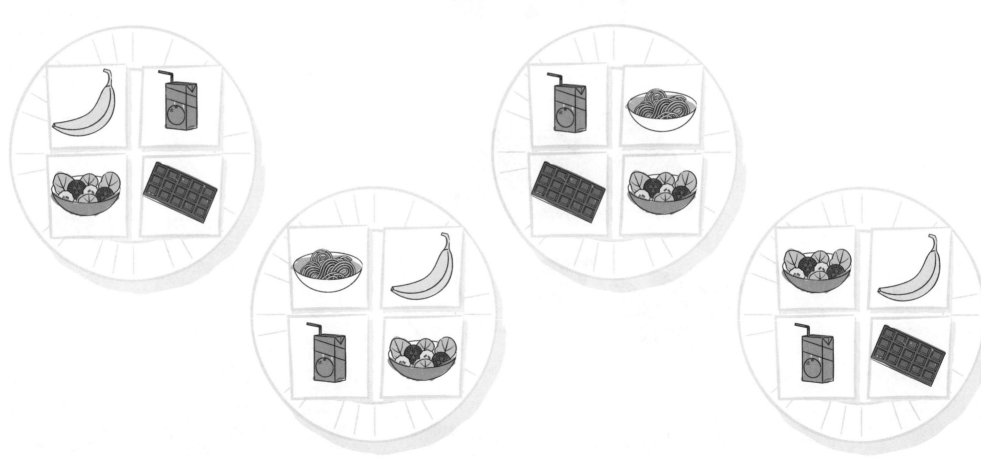

1 Look and match.   **2** 🔊022 Listen and point.

About us Now I know

1 What's different in picture 2? Circle four things.

1 Color for you. Circle for someone else. What's the same?

1 Think of a food for Monkey. Draw.

2 Do you like the story? Color.

1   2   3

1 Count and color the number.

Let's notice things

1 Look and match.

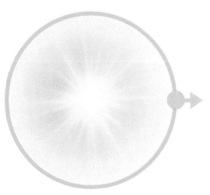

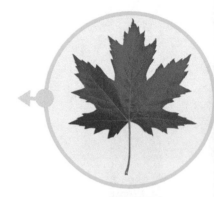

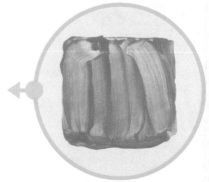

Lesson 1 Concept   **Units 7–9 concept:** observation   **Language focus:** *different, the same*

1 Look around you. Choose one picture and draw what you can see.

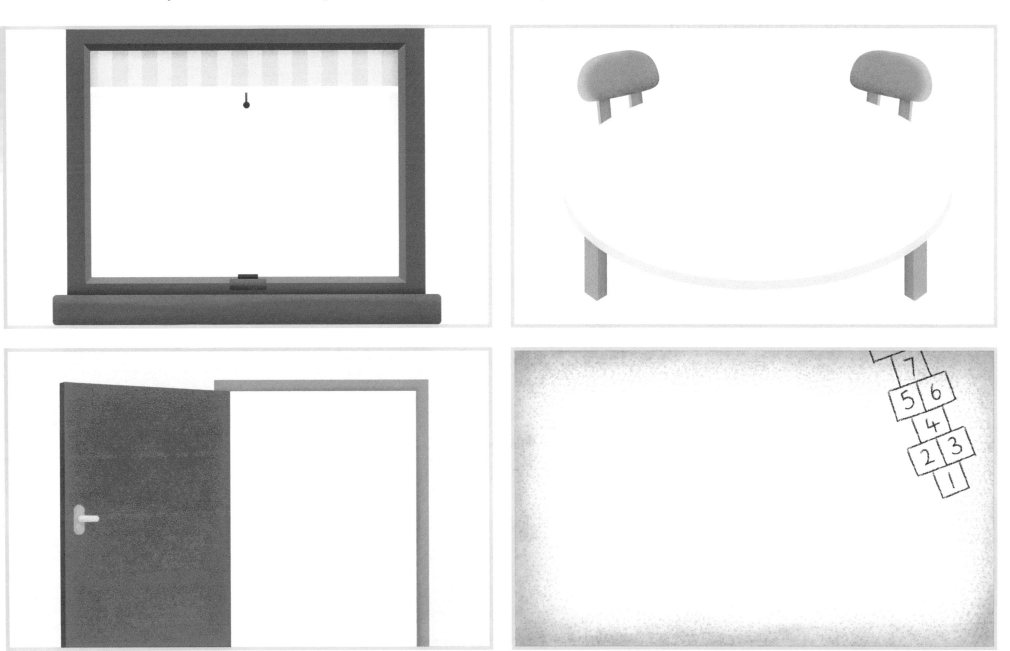

7 What's this?

1 Look, sort, and match.

Lesson 1 Introduction   Unit 7 focus: noticing the shapes and colors of everyday objects

1 🔊 023 Listen and point.　　**2** 🔊 024 Listen again and color.

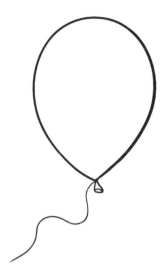   

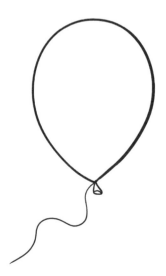   

Language focus: *What's this? It's a/an (orange) teddy bear / monster / balloon / doll.*　Lesson 2 Game　**79**

7

1 Trace and say.

2 Find and color **p**, **q**, and **r**.

p q r

p q

q

r p

r p

q p r

Lesson 3 Phonics   **Language focus:** initial letter sounds *p (purple), q (queen), r (robot)*

1 Do you remember? Look and match. 2 Color the toys to match the story. Say.

   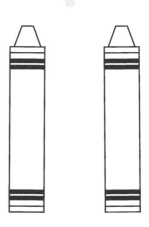

Language focus: *It's my (blue) (robot). Don't worry.* **Lesson 4** Story 81

1 Color the clean room.

Lesson 5 Value — **Value:** be clean — **Language focus:** *What a mess! Let's clean up.*

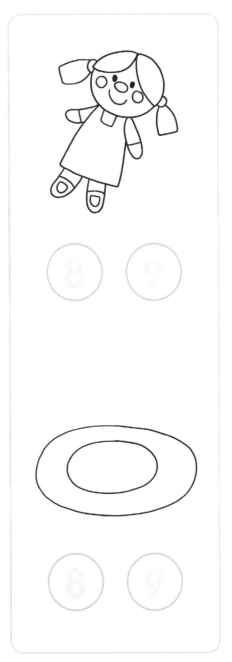

1 Count and color the number.

1 🔊 025 Listen and point. **2** 🔊 026 Listen and trace.

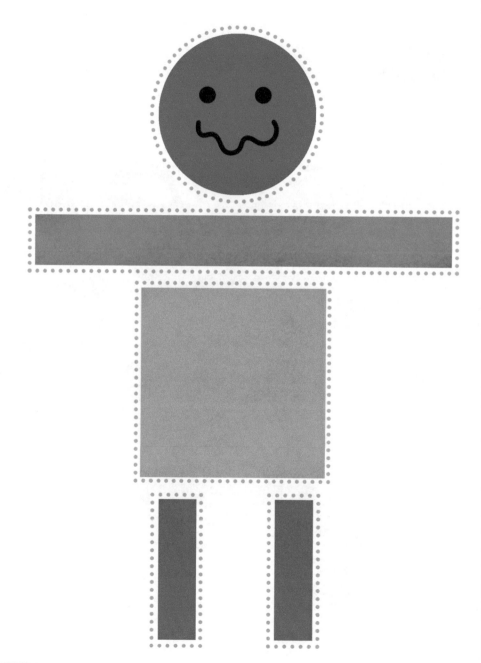

Lesson 7 Song   **Language focus:** *Where's the (green) triangle / circle / rectangle / square? Here it is.*

1 Find the shapes in the painting. Match.

1 Find the shapes in the picture. Color ✓. Which shape is missing?

Lesson 9 Project   **Language focus:** *Look. It's a (square). It's (red).*

1 Look and color.   2 🔊027 Listen and point.

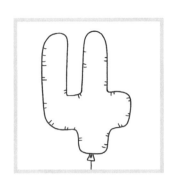

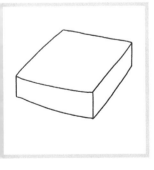

 **What can we see?**

1 Look. Color the circles to match.

1 🔊028 Listen and point. 2 🔊029 Listen again and color ✓.

1 Trace and say.

Ss Tt Uu Vv

2 Connect the letters that are the same.

s ----→ s

t →   u   s

u →   v →   u

t   v

v

1 **What's different in picture 2? Circle five things.**

1 Look and draw 😊 and ☹. **2** Color the 😊 picture.

1 Connect the numbers.

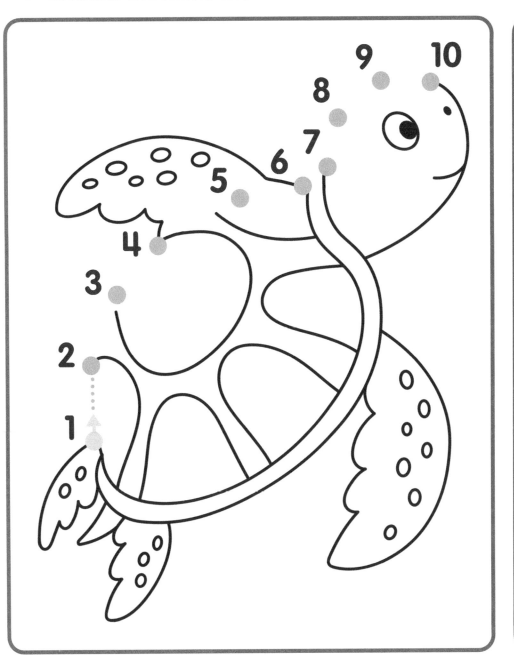

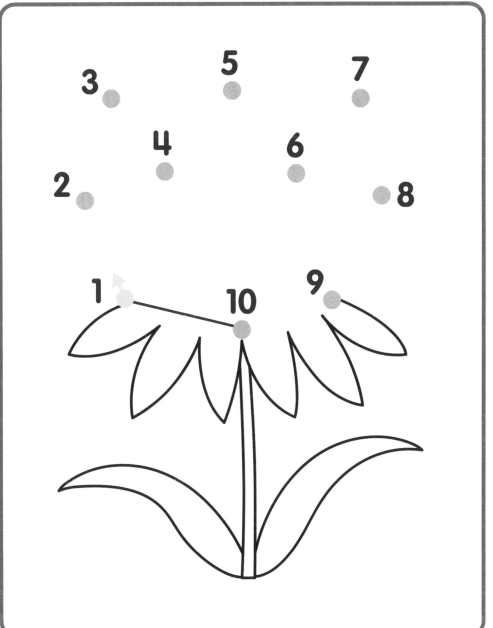

1 ◀))030 Listen and point.   2 ◀))031 Listen again and circle.

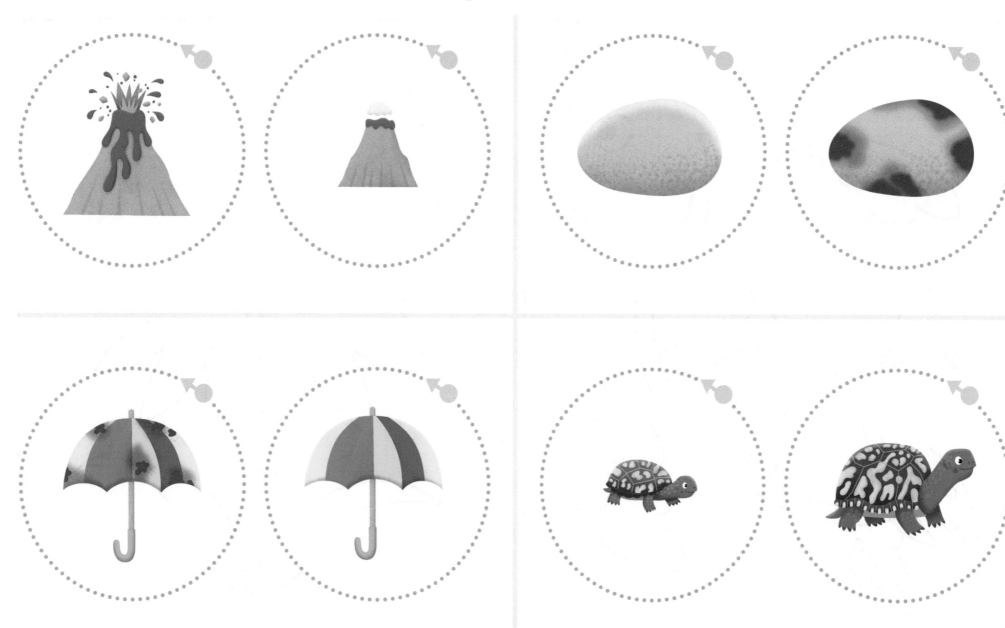

Lesson 7 Song   **Language focus:** *I can see a small / big / dirty / clean (cat).*

1 Find and color the insects.   2 Point and say the colors.

1 Look and match.

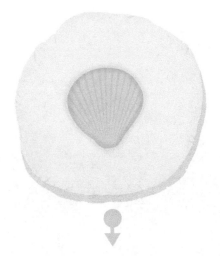
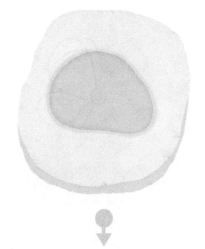

1 Look and match.   2 🔊032 Listen and point.

 # Amazing animals

1 Find and match the animals doing the same thing.   2 Point to the animals you like.

1 🔊033 Listen and point. 2 🔊034 Listen again and color.

1 Trace and say.

2 Find and color **w**, **x**, **y**, and **z**.

Language focus: initial letter sounds *w (window), x (box), y (yellow), z (zebra)*

1 Do you remember? Circle the pictures from the story.

1 Look and draw 🙂 and ☹.

1 Count and circle the number.   2 Point and ask *How many?*

1 🔊035 Listen and color the number.

① ② ③ ④

① ② ③ ④

① ② ③ ④

① ② ③ ④

Lesson 7 Song **Language focus:** *It has a (small) tail / head. It has (two) legs / wings.*

1 Circle the birds with stripes.

2 Draw stripes and color the birds.

1 Look and match.

 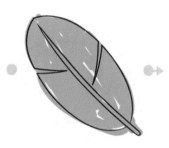 

  Language focus: *This is (a green) feather. I'm a bird. I can fly!*

1 Look and color.   2 🔊036 Listen and point.

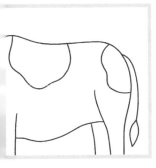

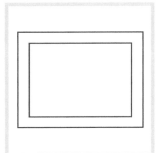

Let's notice things   Now I know

1 Look. Circle the picture that is different.

  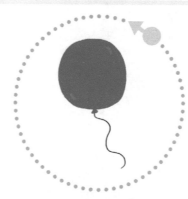 

1 Help the birds. Draw and color.

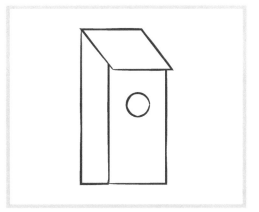

1 Look and color.

2 Do you like the story? Color.

Story time The different duck **Units 7–9 concept:** observation

1 Look. What's next? Draw and color.

OXFORD
UNIVERSITY PRESS

Great Clarendon Street, Oxford, OX2 6DP, United Kingdom

Oxford University Press is a department of the University of Oxford.
It furthers the University's objective of excellence in research, scholarship,
and education by publishing worldwide. Oxford is a registered trade
mark of Oxford University Press in the UK and in certain other countries

© Oxford University Press 2024

The moral rights of the author have been asserted

First published in 2024

2028 2027 2026 2025 2024

10 9 8 7 6 5

ISBN: 978 0 19 486270 7   Little Blue Dot 1 Activity Book

Printed in Great Britain by Bell and Bain Ltd, Glasgow

This book is printed on paper from certified and well-managed sources

ACKNOWLEDGEMENTS

Illustrations by: Ruthine Burton/Alice Williams Literary pp. 38, 39; Claudio
Cerri/Beehive Illustration pp. 7, 17, 21, 27, 43, 48, 53, 60, 63, 79, 89; Estelle
Corke/Advocate pp. 110, 111; James Croft/Advocate pp. 74, 75; Helen Graper/
Beehive Illustration pp. 6, 11, 12, 14, 16, 18, 22, 24, 26, 28, 30, 32, 34, 36, 41,
44, 47, 50, 54, 57, 59, 62, 64, 66, 68, 73, 77, 78, 80, 82, 84, 90, 92, 93, 94, 96, 99,
100; Kevin Payne/Advocate pp. 8, 9, 19, 29, 45, 55, 65, 67, 81, 91, 101; Mark
Ruffle pp. 23, 70, 105, 106, 109; Angelika Scudamore/Advocate pp. 4, 5, 10, 13,
15, 20, 25, 31, 33, 35, 37, 40, 42, 46, 51, 52, 56, 58, 61, 69, 71, 72, 76, 83, 86, 87,
88, 95, 97, 98, 102, 103, 107, 108.

*The publisher would like to thank the following for permission to reproduce
photographs*: 123RF (Bryan Busovicki); Alamy Images (Glasshouse Images,
Red Balloon, Paul Klee, 1922, Solomon R. Guggenheim Museum, Manhattan,
New York City, USA, North America/Peter Barritt); Getty Images (Sigrid
Gombert/Image Source, Nga Nguyen/Moment, Productions/DigitalVision,
Maskot, David Madison/Stone, Sally Anscombe/Stone, Jose Luis Pelaez
Inc/Digital Vision, Rawfile redux/Photodisc, Kevin Lui/Moment, Copyright
Crezalyn Nerona Uratsuji/Moment, Triloks/E+, Indeed/ABSODELS,
Pornpimon Rodchua/iStock, Sally Anscombe/Moment); Shutterstock (Ann
in the UK, Fizkes, Andy Dean Photography, mnimages, Africa Studio, Elena
Chevalier, Monkey Business Images, Artsplav, Quintanilla, Tatiana Popova,
Ruslana Iurchenko, Imtmphoto, Dean Drobot, Irina Wilhauk, Asife, Prostock-
studio, LIGHT_ONLY, Menno Schaefer, Reddogs, Lightspring, Tony Stock,
Mcherevan, Soi7studio, Missleleay1985, Repina Valeriya, MattyPhotog03,
Toon Phasritum, Donikz, Vvoe, Nenov Brothers Images, Buenaventura,
Christan Musat, Aaltair).

Cover: Shutterstock (artjazz, Avesun, Butterfly Hunter, _cz, Kitsana1980,
Kurit afshen, piyaphon, Vandathai).

Title page: Shutterstock (artjazz, Avesun, _cz, Kitsana1980, Kurit afshen,
piyaphon, Vandathai).